Dealing with Drugs

Street Pharma

Jessica Wilkins

Crabtree Publishing Company
www.crabtreebooks.com

Developed and produced by: Plan B Book Packagers
www.planbbookpackagers.com

Editorial director: Ellen Rodger

Art director: Rosie Gowsell-Pattison

Editor: Molly Aloian

Proofreader: Wendy Scavuzzo

Cover design: Margaret Amy Salter

Project coordinator: Kathy Middleton

**Production coordinator and
prepress technician:** Katherine Berti

Print coordinator: Katherine Berti

Photographs:
Front cover: © MBI / Alamy; Title page: Monkey
Business Images/Shutterstock.com; p. 6: Alex
Hubenov/Shutterstock.com; p. 8: Artur Gabrysiak/
Shutterstock.com; p. 9: Arcady/Shutterstock.com;
p. 11: Martin Haas/Shutterstock.com; p. 12: Natalia
Bratslavsky/Shutterstock.com; p. 15: Ibooo7/
Shutterstock.com; p. 16: Luna Vandoorne/
Shutterstock.com; p. 17: Jordache/Shutterstock.com;
p. 20: Greg Dragon/Shutterstock.com; p. 22:
Squareplum/Shutterstock.com; p. 23: Dedyukhin
Dmitry/Shutterstock.com; p. 24: dny3d/
Shutterstock.com; p. 26: Alexander Chaikin/
Shutterstock.com; p. 28: Roman Sigaev/
Shutterstock.com; p. 30: Andrejs Pidjass/
Shutterstock.com; p. 32: Eugenio Marongiu/
Shutterstock.com; p. 33: Tupungato/
Shutterstock.com; p. 34: Urmoments /
Shutterstock.com; p. 36: Pinkcandy/
Shutterstock.com; p. 37: Olemac/Shutterstock.com;
p. 39: Creatista/ Shutterstock.com; p. 40: Golden
Pixels LLC/Shutterstock.com; p. 42: Paul Matthew

Library and Archives Canada Cataloguing in Publication

Wilkins, Jessica
  Street pharma / Jessica Wilkins.

(Dealing with drugs)
Includes index.
Issued also in electronic formats.
ISBN 978-0-7787-5512-8 (bound).--ISBN 978-0-7787-5519-7 (pbk.)

  1. Drug abuse--Juvenile literature. 2. Medication abuse--
Juvenile literature. I. Title. II. Series: Dealing with drugs (St.
Catharines, Ont.)

HV5809.5.W54 2011   j362.29'9   C2011-905637-2

Library of Congress Cataloging-in-Publication Data

Wilkins, Jessica.
  Street pharma / Jessica Wilkins.
    p. cm. -- (Dealing with drugs)
  Includes bibliographical references and index.
  ISBN 978-0-7787-5512-8 (reinforced library binding : alk. paper)
-- ISBN 978-0-7787-5519-7 (pbk. : alk. paper) -- ISBN 978-1-4271-
8827-4 (electronic pdf : alk. paper) -- ISBN 978-1-4271-9730-6
(electronic html : alk. paper)
  1. Drug abuse--Juvenile literature. I. Title. II. Series.

  HV5809.5.W55 2012
  362.29'9--dc23
                                                    2011032622

Crabtree Publishing Company

www.crabtreebooks.com   1-800-387-7650

Printed in the U.S.A./112011/JA20111018

Published in Canada
Crabtree Publishing
616 Welland Ave.
St. Catharines, Ontario
L2M 5V6

Published in the United States
Crabtree Publishing
PMB 59051
350 Fifth Avenue, 59th Floor
New York, New York 10118

Published in the United Kingdom
Crabtree Publishing
Maritime House
Basin Road North, Hove
BN41 1WR

Published in Australia
Crabtree Publishing
3 Charles Street
Coburg North
VIC 3058

Facts & Stats

- Prescription and over the counter (OTC) drugs are the drugs most commonly abused by high school students after marijuana. One in five young people abuse prescription meds.

- Prescription and over the counter drugs make up six of the top ten drugs most abused drugs by high school students.

- Long-term effects of abusing over the counter drugs include addiction, insomnia, high blood pressure, coma, and even death.

- A U.S. national survey on drug use and health revealed that, in the last month, an estimated 6.9 million persons, or 2.8 percent of the population, had used a prescription medication that was not prescribed to them.

Introduction
When Helpful Becomes Harmful

Prescription drugs and over the counter (OTC) medications are helpful in treating a number of different health issues such as pain, **depression**, or an inability to concentrate. They are also a dangerous and growing source of **addiction** in people who take them for other reasons—to get high, to feel more relaxed, or forget their troubles.

Most doctors think carefully before prescribing medications, because prescription medications are powerful substances. Using **meds** not prescribed to you, or using them in a dosage or way other than what was intended, is considered **misuse** and drug abuse. Prescription and OTC meds are easily found in household medicine cabinets and on drugstore shelves. This means they are often the first drugs young people experiment with. You may believe taking them to get high or get an edge is safer than using street drugs. It isn't. Using meds you don't need is just as dangerous as using street drugs.

In this book, you'll learn what prescription drug abuse is, how to avoid using drugs, as well as what addiction is, and how to help yourself, or a friend who is "hooked."

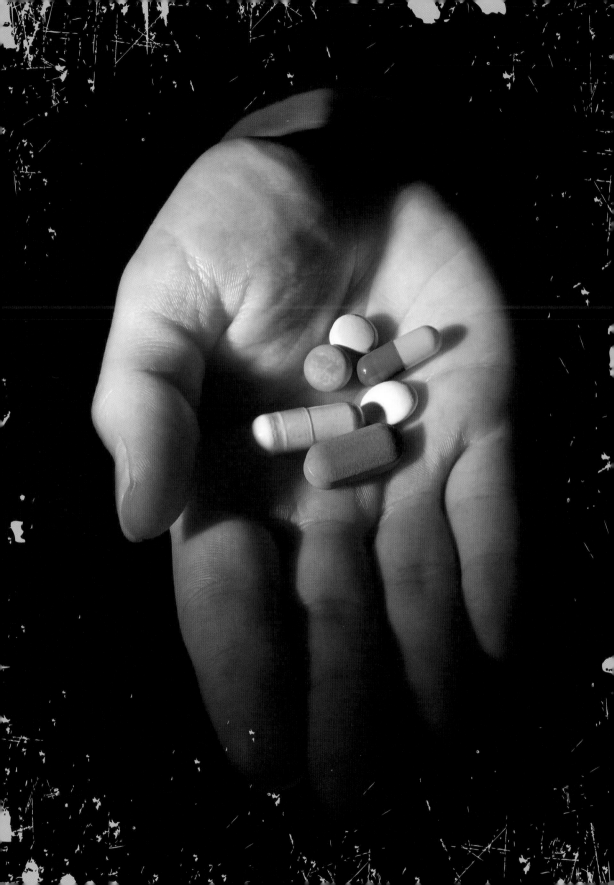

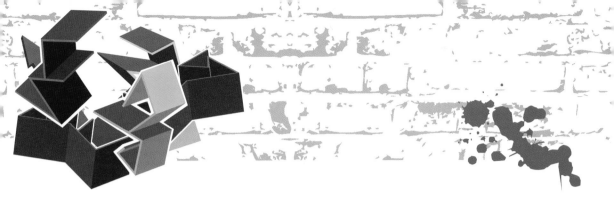

Chapter 1
What's the Big Deal?

Prescription medications and over the counter (OTC) drugs help people control pain or manage other health conditions. They are intended to make life easier for people who are suffering. Drugs, whether they are prescribed by a doctor, sold legally in stores, or bought illegally on the street, are powerful substances that can affect our bodies and minds in intended and unintended ways.

Some people think that because prescription and over the counter drugs are legal, they are safe for anyone to use. A few painkillers taken from your grandma's pill bottles can't hurt can they? Actually, they can hurt—and they can kill. These drugs are medications, or substances used for medical treatment of specific diseases and medical conditions. They are only safe when they are used under a doctor's care, by the person for whom the medication is prescribed. Even when prescribed by a doctor, some medications can become addictive or can **react** with other drugs, with alcohol, and even with certain foods. Using drugs in a way that is different from the way they are intended to be used is dangerous.

How Medications Help

All medications, whether prescribed by a doctor or bought over the counter, alter the way our bodies and minds work. Pain medications are intended to help a person with an injury or illness live normally by blocking pain messages in the body's **cells**. Sleeping pills help people diagnosed with **insomnia** fall sleep by producing a calming effect on the brain. Medications that treat **anxiety** or depression may help people with severe anxiety feel more at ease by calming the body's **central nervous system** or reducing activity in the brain. Drugs prescribed for conditions such as **Attention Deficit Hyperactivity Disorder** (ADHD) stimulate different parts of the brain to help people concentrate and focus. Drugs are designed to help with symptoms of specific health conditions. Over the counter cold medications for example, are intended to help ease the pain of a cold and reduce nasal congestion.

All drugs have *side effects* and risks—even when prescribed for a specific illness or condition. Doctors and pharmacists inform patients about how to take medications safely.

How Meds Can Harm

Taking any kind of med—from aspirin to prescribed drugs—may not seem like a big deal. Prescription and OTC meds are legal, and relatively easy to get your hands on, so they must be safe right? Wrong. Every medication has a purpose. If used improperly, or if taken by someone who does not have the condition for which the drugs were prescribed, medications can be addictive and deadly. They can make it difficult for a person to function normally and can even permanently damage organs such as the kidneys, liver, heart, or brain.

Abusing meds can harm your body in many ways. Some ways we know about, and some we don't. Sometimes those effects don't become apparent until many years later. Taking meds intended for people diagnosed with ADHD for example, may lead to increased heart and breathing rates, tremors, or uncontrolled shaking, and vomiting. In severe cases, they can even cause heart attack and death. A drug may not have the same affect on every person because they are designed to alter individual brain chemistry.

Why Do Drugs?

There are a lot of reasons why someone might abuse prescription or OTC meds. Some may experiment with medications found at home because they want to feel different, to forget about their worries, or numb emotional pain. Prescription and OTC meds offer an escape, or a way to feel less unhappy or anxious, or just not "feel" at all. Some people use drugs because they like the sensation of being high. Others do it because their friends are doing it.

Feeling Lost

Difficulties at home, being bullied at school, or struggling with a learn disability are all things that can make life difficult. Sometimes, adolescents and teens feel helpless and like things aren't ever going to change. They may start using drugs as a way of escaping and feeling better. The thing is, prescription drug abuse usually starts out slowly. Maybe you just take some pills before going to a party, or as a way to "zone-out" after a rough day. Maybe you use prescription drugs when you feel like you're in **crisis** and are overwhelmed. Over time, you might notice that you want or need to take these drugs more often. For example, instead of just taking drugs when you're feeling like there's no way out, you take them when you wake up so that you can get through the day.

What Is Drug Abuse?

Drug or substance abuse is the harmful use of a, drug such as a medication, without a prescription. It is also using a drug in a way other than how it was prescribed, for the feeling it causes or the experience it provides.

Abusing Drugs

Prescription drug abuse occurs when someone takes a med that was prescribed for someone else, or when they take it in a larger **dose** than what was prescribed. OTC drug abuse occurs when someone takes a medication in a larger amount then what is recommended, or takes it for a reason other than for what the medication is intended. For example, taking a cough medicine that contains **dextromethorphan** to get high when you don't have a cough. Abuse can include taking a friend's or relative's medication to get high, to help with studying, or to feel less pain.

Just a Little Won't Hurt...

Medications were made to help us feel better, so taking more medication, or combining medications should makes us feel even better, right? Not so! Taking a drug in any way other then how it was intended is called misuse. Doubling the recommended dosage of a prescription or OTC med won't make you feel twice as good, and can instead cause serious harm.

Combining drugs for a stronger high, or to come down from a high, and not following medication instructions, are recipes for disaster.

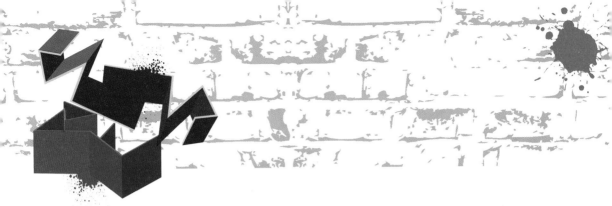

Chapter 2
Legal and Available

Each day, approximately 2,000 teens throughout the United States use a prescription drug for the first time without a doctor's supervision. According to the National Institute on Drug Abuse (NIDA), eight of the 14 drugs most frequently abused by adolescents are prescription and over the counter medications. There are many reasons for this. Prescription and OTC drugs are easy for adolescents to find in their homes. Most adolescents also think these drugs are safer because they haven't been produced in back alley drug labs. Most don't even think frequent or regular use of these drugs constitutes drug abuse.

There are a number of different ways that someone can get their hands on prescription or OTC meds. Some adolescents and teens raid their family's medicine cabinet, or they get them from a friend or relative. Some purchase prescription medication on the street from someone who is selling them illegally. OTC drugs can be bought off the shelves of the nearest pharmacy, supermarket, or convenience store. Prescription meds can also be ordered over the Internet.

Easy to Abuse

We know that prescription and OTC drugs are easy to find and easy to abuse but, even when used properly under a doctor's direction, these drugs can have side effects and unintended results. Side effects are conditions such as blurred vision, or stomach upset that occur as a result of using the medication. Some side effects are very serious. Unintended results are complications that result from using the drug in a proper manner. Some drugs, for example, help people cope with pain but they may be so strong that misuse or overuse damages vital organs such as the liver or kidneys.

Some prescription drugs are designed for long-term use by people with **chronic** conditions. Their bodies adapt to using the drug. Under a doctor's care, the medication type and dosage are tailored to the needs of the patient, so that they don't use too much. Other medications are meant only for short-term use. Have you ever noticed the directions on the back of an over the counter pain reliever? They give the recommended dosages for adults and warnings not to exceed that dosage unless directed by a physician. These drugs are supposed to be used as directed and not in combination with other drugs or alcohol.

How Common?

Painkillers are among the drugs most commonly abused by teens after tobacco, alcohol, and marijuana.

Brand Name

The most commonly abused prescription and over the counter drugs are divided into categories based on the different effects they have on the brain and body. They include opiods, or painkillers, central nervous system depressants, or depressants, and stimulants. Within each class of these medications, there are a number of different kinds of drugs which have a brand name, and a street name. Brand names are the names that medical doctors and pharmacists use to describe different medications made by pharmaceutical companies. You may have heard some of the brand names from your doctor, or from advertisements on television or in magazines.

Store shelves are stocked with brand name medications that treat everything from headaches to colds and fevers. These products are legal to buy, but can still be dangerous if used improperly.

Street Name Street Use

Prescription and OTC drugs also have "street" names, which are short forms or nicknames they are called by users of the drug. For example, the drug Ritalin prescribed for people with ADHD is the brand name used for the chemical medication methylphenidate. Ritalin is also known by the street name Vitamin R, the smart drug, or skippy. There are a lot of different names that are used to describe the same medication. The names can also change depending on who you are talking to, such as your doctor, friends, or parents.

A street name tells you nothing about the drug, what it is used for legally, or its dangers.

Serious Stuff

When your kid brother was prescribed Ritalin for Attention Deficit Hyperactivity Disorder (ADHD), it was intended to help him focus on tasks and control his behavior. His doctor would have given him, and your parents, instruction on how much medication to take and when to take it. The same goes for your uncle with the bad back. His medication was prescribed to him to help him live with terrible pain. His doctor monitors his dosage (the amount he takes each time he takes it), and controls his ongoing use of the drug. The drug itself may even be time-released, which means the pain-killing properties are not released all at once, but over a period of time so that the pain is controlled without making the patient high.

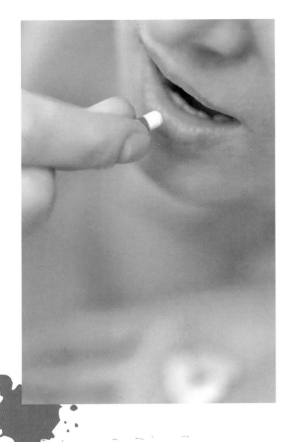

Prescription and over the counter medications are used by following the directions on the packaging or the doctor's instructions on a pill bottle. OTC drugs are safe when used as directed to help treat common illnesses. The fact that a drug is readily available does not mean it is always safe. There are serious risks to taking any drug. The risks depend on what you use, how much you use it, and how you use it.

Opioids

Types	Street Names	Recommended Use in General	Effects in General
Painkillers such as OxyContin Percocet Dilaudid Demerol Methadone Morphine Codeine Vicodin	oxy, OC, percs, dillies, demmies, juice, dope Cody, vikes	Post-surgery pain relief Managing long-term pain Managing acute pain	Pain relief, drowsiness, constipation, decreased breathing rate, coma, death. Potential for dependence and addiction.

Over the Counter

Types	Street Names	Recommended Use	Effects
Dextroamphetamine (DXM)	Dex	Suppresses coughs due to colds	Decreased control over movement, numbness, nausea, vomiting, increased heart rate and blood pressure.
Diet pills	Xenadrine Liporexall Hoodia	Aids weight loss	High blood pressure, dehydration, heart attack, coma, death.
Sexual Performance Enhancers	Cialis Viagra	Treats erectile dysfunction in men	Heart problems including increased blood pressure and heart attack.

Stimulants

Types	Street Names in General	Recommended Use	Effects
Ritalin Concerta Adderall	Skippy, the smart drug, Vitamin R, bennies, black beauties, speed, uppers, wake-ups	Prescribed to treat Attention Deficit Hyperactivity Disorder, narcolepsy (a sleep disorder), and depression.	Elevated blood pressure; increased heart rate; increased respiration; decreased appetite; increased alertness, concentration, and energy.

CNS Depressants

Types	Street Names in General	Recommended Use	Effects
Valium Xanax Klonopin Ativan Ambien Sonata Dalmane Lectopam Versed	Yellows, yellow jackets, candy, downers, sleeping pills, tranks, zombie pills	Prescribed to help alleviate anxiety, panic attacks, sleep disorders.	A "sleepy" or uncoordinated feeling, drowsiness, seizures during withdrawal. Users can become addicted physically and psychologically.

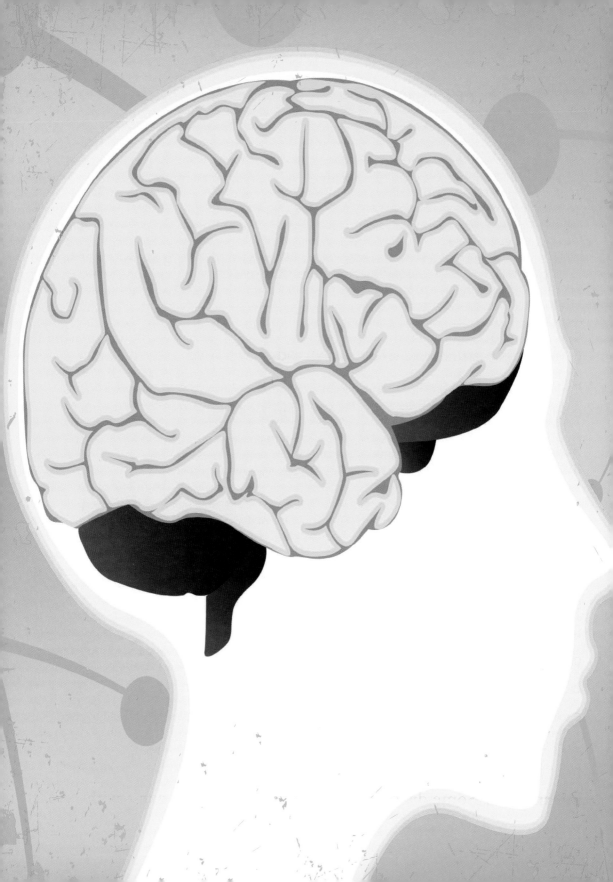

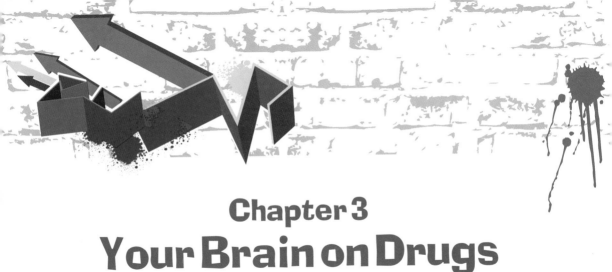

Chapter 3
Your Brain on Drugs

The brain is a very complex machine. It weighs just three pounds (1.36 kg) but it is the center of the body's nervous system—an information processing system that includes the spinal cord and nerves. Different parts of the brain perform different body functions. Without a properly functioning brain, it would be impossible to walk, talk, breath, think, remember, or even live.

Our brains control so many things, yet they are often ignored. Brains are made up of nerve cells called neurons. We have about 100 billion of them that function as electrochemical signal transmitters. Like computers, brain neurons carry information and pass messages on to each other. Some neurons control muscle movement, and some carry messages to other cells in our skin, organs, and glands. Neurons transmit or communicate messages from nerve cell to nerve cell chemically in a process called neurotransmission. Drugs are chemicals that alter how the brain's nerve cells or neurons, send, receive, and process information. Some drugs do this temporarily. Some can—with repeated use or misuse—permanently alter your brain function.

Brainwork

All drugs, whether they are legal or illegal, change the brain's natural or normal function. Sometimes these changes are necessary to prevent pain or help a person live normally with a medical condition. Prescription and OTC drugs are designed to be used a certain way. For example, an OTC aspirin or acetylsalicylic acid (ASA) is designed to reduce pain and fever by blocking the brain's chemical signal that causes the sensation of pain. ASA specifically targets chemicals called prostaglandins that are released by cells in the body. ASA is seemingly harmless, but even so-called harmless drugs can be harmful if used repeatedly or improperly. ASA is a pill that, when swallowed, enters the body's digestive system and is distributed throughout the bloodstream. It is then spread throughout the body, not just to the areas where there is pain. Health studies show long term **excessive** use of even a helpful OTC drug such as ASA can lead to health problems such as stomach bleeding—a serious and life-threatening condition.

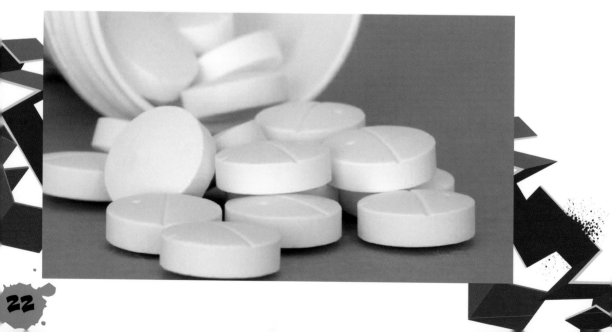

Your Brain and Body on Opioids

Opioids such as the brand name medications OxyContin (oxycodone), Vicodin (hydrocodone), Demerol (meperidine) or Percocet (oxycodone and acetaminophen) are strong painkillers. They work by attaching to special **receptors** in your brain, spinal cord, stomach, intestines, and other organs, and reducing their ability to **perceive** pain. Doctors prescribe opioids to help manage regular or chronic pain, but opioids also affect the parts of your brain that respond to pleasure, often leading to increased feelings of pleasure. This is why many recreational users like opioids—they give them a pleasant buzz, or at least they do at first. The problem is opioids are addictive. Over time, a person needs more to relieve pain or get high. This is called developing a tolerance. Opioids also slow the body's respiration or breathing. When used in large quantities, as they are when someone develops a tolerance, they can lead to coma, particularly if the drugs are combined with alcohol.

Opioid abuse can cause mood changes, and a decrease in cognitive function, or the ability to process thoughts, understand ideas, and remember things.

How Depressants Work

Central nervous system (CNS) depressants are prescription drugs used to treat conditions such as epilepsy, anxiety, and sleep disorders. They include drugs such as sodium pentobarbital (Nembutal), diazepam (Valium), alprazolam (Xanax), and zolpidem (Ambien). CNS depressants come in pill or capsule form and work by slowing activity in your brain, and slowing communication between your brain and other parts of your body. They affect brain cells that control activity inside your brain and body and, when their activity decreases, it can lead to feelings of being calm or tired. This effect is helpful for people who live with **anxiety disorders** or who have extreme difficulty sleeping. They can also help relax someone who is having a **panic attack**, relax by treating the physical symptoms of their panic such as a racing heart. Too much of these drugs can slow down important functions in the brain and lead to confusion, slowed breathing, coma, or death. Abusing CNS depressants can cause seizures, which occur when there is suddenly more activity in your brain after discontinuing use.

Depressants

Depressants are sometimes called forget pills or zombie pills because of their ability to relax people.

24

Your Brain on Stimulants

Stimulants such as methylphenidate (Ritalin and Concerta) and amphetamine dextroamphetamine (Adderall) are prescription meds used to treat ADD/ADHD and narcolepsy, a sleep disorder in which people fall asleep at **inappropriate** times. Stimulants work by increasing brain activity and changing the way nerve cells or neurons, transmit or send messages to each other. Stimulants act to calm people with ADHD and help them focus. People who don't need these drugs to function use them to feel more alert, awake, or to decrease their appetite. Some people report feeling a sense of euphoria, or great joy or happiness, when using them. This is due in part to the stimulants causing a buildup and release of dopamine in the brain. Dopamine is a neurotransmitter naturally released in the brain when something good happens.

Short and Long Term

Stimulants elevate blood pressure and heart rate and can cause nausea, blurred vision, and confusion. When used repeatedly by people for whom they were not prescribed, stimulants can be addictive. They can also lead to strange and even violent behavior, and feelings of panic and paranoia. Stimulant abuse affects the way the brain responds to pleasure—making it difficult to even experience the same high or boost the user once felt with the drug. They then just feel flat or depressed.

Chapter 4
Pharmaceutical History

Many historians believe that humans have had a long history of drug use. Researchers have even found **paraphernalia** used to make drugs in prehistoric caves. Early drugs, made from wild plants, herbs, and seeds were used to relieve pain or bring on trance-like states for religious ceremonies. The modern drug industry has its origins in the early 1800s, when "druggists" set up shops selling potions that helped (or claimed to help) a number of **ailments**. Most of these potions were made by hand in small batches or by small companies, and their effectiveness varied. Some were even toxic. There were few laws that guaranteed the drugs being sold were safe or effective.

Pharmaceutical Safety

A mass poisoning from the use of an untested **sulfa** drug killed 100 people in 1937 and forced the United States government to pass the Federal Food, Drug, and Cosmetic Act. This law required pharmaceutical drug makers to test their products and provide the test results to the Food and Drug Administration before they can be sold to the public.

What's What

As scientists learned more about the way medications could help and hurt us, even more laws were created. These laws distinguished between prescription, over the counter, and illegal drugs. The FDA is a branch of the U.S. federal government that helps to monitor and test new drugs. Most countries have similar organizations and similar pharmaceutical testing laws. They decide which drugs should be available only by prescription under the supervision of a doctor, and which are safe and effective to be used by following label directions over the counter. The world of prescription and OTC medication has evolved into a large industry that makes a lot of money, and has helped to improve the lives of many people.

There was no U.S. federal regulation governing the safety and effectiveness of drugs at all until the 1906 Food and Drugs Act. Without laws to stop them, people sold phony remedies that were often dangerous or harmful to people.

Fighting Drug Misuse

The pharmaceutical industry makes billions of dollars each year producing and selling drugs. The process of creating a new drug, from the idea stage through to testing and public use, is a long one. It takes many years and a lot of money to make a new prescription or OTC drug—about $1.7 billion by some estimates. With that kind of investment, drug companies do not want to pull drugs from the market. They also don't want "off market" uses of prescription meds to taint the reputation of their drugs used in **legitimate** ways. Once a new drug is created, it is tested over and over to make sure it is safe for people to use.

Drug companies also change drug formulations to try to end **intentional** misuse or abuse. For example, the makers of the painkiller OxyContin **reformulated** the drug in the U.S. to help prevent misuse. OxyContin is a control-release painkiller in pill form the was designed to be swallowed. Controlled release drugs are designed to give continuous relief from pain. Addicts misuse the drug by crushing it, injecting the crushed pill, or chewing or snorting it so that the oxycodone narcotic in the drug is released quickly for a high. The reformulated drug cannot be crushed or chewed to dissolve more medication. The pills now turn to gel when crushed with water, making it difficult to inject but still not entirely impossible to misuse.

Pill Mills

Pill mills are what police call clinics, doctors, or pharmacies that prescribe powerful meds for nonmedical reasons.

Chapter 5
Dependence and Addiction

Doctors and psychologists define addiction as a physical and or psychological dependence on a substance. Most people who work in the fields of addiction research or treatment believe addiction is a chronic disease, or something that can be treated but never entirely cured. Being dependent or addicted to a drug means quitting it isn't a simple matter of just stopping. Some people don't even recognize that they are dependent on a drug. Some know it and **rationalize** it. They may say things like "I don't have a problem, I just like to get high once in a while," or "I'm not hurting anyone." If "once in a while" is a couple of times a week, it is a pretty safe bet a person is dependent on the drug.

There are many different signs that you or someone you know may be dependent on or addicted to prescription or OTC drugs. One of the most common is feeling like you NEED to have the drug. This is called a craving. Other signs of drug addiction include changes in mood, losing or gaining weight, or lack of interest in the things that you used to enjoy.

Physically Addicted

Addiction affects your body, as well as the way you think and feel. When a person is dependent on a drug, it means that their body physically needs to have the drug in their system. When they do not have the drug, their body takes notice. They may become physically sick, going through **withdrawal** until they get more of it. Someone who is dependent on a prescription stimulant such as Adderall can experience withdrawal symptoms that include long periods of sleep, irritability, feeling depressed, convulsions, and disorientation. Someone who is experiencing withdrawal from an opioid such as Percocet may experience slow breathing, clammy skin, tremors, chills, nausea, and irritability.

It's not a good idea to quit on your own. Seek medical help to kick your addiction.

Psychological Cravings

It is possible to be psychologically addicted, or to mentally crave a drug, without experiencing the physical symptoms of dependence and withdrawal. What this means is that you don't have to experience withdrawal (feeling sick when you don't take the drug) or physically crave the drug, to be addicted to it. Doctors and drug counselors note that addiction often means someone continues to use a drug despite experiencing problems in their behavior and their relationships as a result of using it. This could mean getting in trouble in school, failing or lower grades, getting arrested, or losing friends. Addicts don't do drugs just because it makes them feel good. Sometimes the drugs they do make them feel wretched, but they keep chasing the high or the feeling they felt when they first did the drug, even if that means a higher dose, a riskier way of taking it, or combining the drug with other drugs or alcohol.

More Risks

Teens who abuse prescription drugs before the age of 16 are at greater risk of dependence in later life.

When Addiction Runs the Show

In the beginning when people start taking drugs, they may feel like they help them escape from their problems or uncomfortable feelings. At first, the drugs may make them feel good, help them to relax, or help them concentrate. All of these factors make it even easier to become mentally dependent or addicted to drugs. When addiction is running the show, it can make people act in ways they would never have acted before they started abusing drugs. They may steal money to be able to buy more of the drug, or steal the drug from someone's medicine cabinet. They may hurt the people who love them, or say or do things they would otherwise never do. When you are dependent or addicted to a drug, you may be angry and irritable when going through withdrawal or when you haven't used, then happy and energetic once you've used again.

Addiction is a roller coaster, for the addict and those close to them.

Chasing a High

Parents and teachers warn about how drugs destroy lives. Turn on the television and you can find any number of shows—both fiction reality—that graphically depict the brutal affects of addiction. Addicts are usually shown at their worst—as stumbling, violent, or confused. Addicts can seem to function well, too. They may be able to "keep it together" for awhile, but often their body's need for higher doses puts them in great danger of risky behavior and overdosing. Overdosing happens when someone takes too much of a drug. Pretty simple, right? Not quite. Accidental overdose can happen the first time someone uses a drug. It also happens quite frequently to addicts. If they are lucky, they will be able to feel the signs and get emergency help. Depending on the drug, prescription and OTC drug addicts may feel tingling in their fingers or toes, or they may get the shakes, feel sick to their stomach, feel agitated, or find it hard to breath. If not caught in time and dealt with in a hospital, an overdose will lead to coma, brain damage, or death.

Risky Business

Addiction can lead to an increase in other risky behaviors. People behave differently when they are high. They often worry less, or act without thinking. This happens because many drugs disrupt the parts of the brain that help people to reason and make decisions. As a result, addicts may be more likely to like steal, drive under the influence, or have unprotected sex. They are also more likely to mix different drugs and alcohol, which makes overdose more likely.

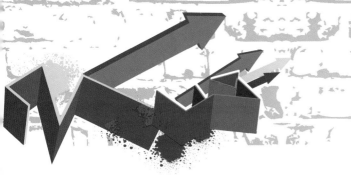

Chapter 6
Seeking Help

If you're abusing prescription drugs, or are addicted to them, you've probably been keeping a lot of secrets. You might be stealing to get your hands on drugs, lying to your parents and friends about taking them, or trying to hide the signs and symptoms from friends and adults who might be concerned about you.

Keeping so many secrets can be exhausting, and it might make you feel really isolated and alone. Secrets can be dangerous. When the people who care about us don't know what is going on, they can't help. Not letting safe adults in your life know that you are having a hard time can put you at greater risk for hurting yourself or someone else. If you isolate yourself and do drugs alone, there is a greater chance that no one will be around to help if you overdose.

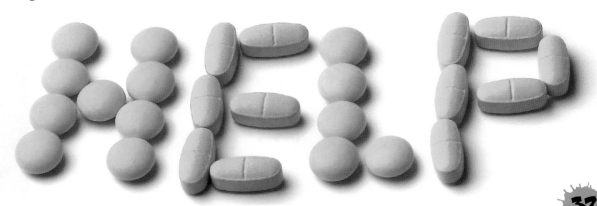

Let the Secret Out

Talking to someone about your secrets is the first step in getting help. It's also one of the most difficult. It may be really difficult to let someone know that you are having a hard time. You may feel ashamed or guilty that you have been abusing a drug. You may feel bad about some things that you have done or said while high. You may even feel that no one cares anyway. That is why it is important to consider who to reach out to for help, and how you can go about doing it.

Disclosure—the "D" Word

Disclosure is the word we use to describe the act of talking to someone about what is going on with you. It's the step you take to share some of your secrets with someone whom you can trust. There are important reasons to disclose to a trusted adult or friend that you are abusing prescription or over the counter drugs. Carefully consider who to share with. You want to make sure that the person you talk to will be willing and able to listen, and help you without judging you. Some examples of people you might talk to about drug abuse and addiction include your doctor, counselor, teacher, a parent, or another close friend or family member.

Emergency Help

If you are scared and don't know where to go for help, look for a suicide prevention hotline. Suicide prevention hotlines can help connect you with local crisis centers and places to get help with an addiction. You don't have to be considering suicide to ask them for help.

Talk It Out

Talking to someone about abusing prescription or OTC drugs, or about addiction to drugs can be a really difficult conversation. It's important to carefully think about whom you might talk to, as well as what you might say. Sometimes it can be easier to talk to a stranger about drug abuse and addiction than it would be to talk to a family member or friend. If you have no one you trust, or you just want to talk to someone who doesn't know you, you can phone a drug addiction hotline. There are a number of hotlines that

exist exactly for that reason. These hotlines are staffed by professional and compassionate counselors who will listen to you. They can also help you get connected to resources and services in your area.

You might be surprised who will help you when you ask them to.

Thinking About the Good and Bad

There will be positive and negative consequences to disclosing. Some of the positive effects include feeling less isolated and alone, having someone to talk to, taking the first step toward treatment and recovery, and feeling relieved that you don't have to keep the secret anymore. There are also some risks to disclosing drug abuse and addiction that are important to consider. The person you choose to talk to may not be understanding or **empathetic**. You may also need to face the consequences of risky or dangerous things you have done while high. Be prepared. This may mean that you need to own up to stealing drugs or money, or that your parents or guardians might find out that you have been skipping school. It is important that you consider both the benefits and the risks of talking to someone about your struggles before you make the decision to disclose. This will be a very personal decision.

Disclosure carries risks, such as rejection, but it can be rewarding too. Often, people want to help.

How to Help a Friend

It may be difficult to watch your friend struggling with drug dependence and addiction. It can be even more difficult to tell them that you think they might be in over their head. If you believe that your friend is abusing prescription or over the counter drugs, or if you think they may be addicted, you can help them by encouraging them to get in touch with addiction and counseling resources. It takes a lot of courage to confront them. It is important for you to know that you can't make your friend get help. The most helpful thing you can do for your friend is to let them know that you care, and will do what you can to help them find help.

Getting help is an important decision that your friend will need to come to on his or her own. Your friend may even say to you that their drug abuse isn't a big deal, or they may deny that they have a problem. This is a pretty common response. You don't have to wait until the problem gets worse to talk to them about it. Some signs and symptoms that you might see in a friend who is abusing prescription or over the counter drugs include

- **changes in mood**
- **getting high on a regular basis (this may be daily, weekly, or a few times a month such as weekend binges)**
- **not showing up for school, or skipping class to get high and lying about drug use**
- **showing little interest in activities they used to enjoy**
- **borrowing or stealing money to buy drugs**

Chapter 7
Treatment and Recovery

Quitting drugs isn't easy and it isn't simple. It isn't a matter of just wanting to be clean. Drug treatment and recovery is a multi-stage, often lifelong process that involves treating the physical and psychological parts of addiction. It also involves addressing or talking about the underlying issues or problems that might have led to drug misuse and abuse. It requires a lot of effort and support. For many young people struggling with addiction and drug abuse, taking the very first step is the most difficult—the decision to make a change and ask for support.

If you are struggling with addiction, and feeling as though you are drowning in problems, it may seem that living a drug-free life is an impossible goal. It is possible to live without drugs with the right support. There are many different roads toward a drug-free life, but all of them are slow and can be challenging. No matter which way you work toward recovery, there will be pitfalls, setbacks, and most likely, **relapses**. This is simply the nature of trying to make a very difficult life change.

Treatment Options and Plans

Unfortunately, there is no magic wand that takes away physical or psychological cravings for drugs. There is also no one fool-proof drug treatment program that works for everyone. Everyone who is struggling with addiction will have different needs and experiences. Treatment should address more than the physical and psychological dependence on your drug of choice. It should deal with your whole life, including school, relationships, and family. Many addicts have painful experiences in their past, including physical or sexual abuse, that contributed to their drug abuse. For these people, coming off drugs can bring the memory of these experiences to the forefront. Drug treatment for them will mean **acknowledging** their pain and finding other ways to cope with it.

Where to Turn

There are many places you can turn to for help. The first step is coming off drugs, or detoxing. This means withdrawal, which can make people sick, depressed, or even suicidal. Some drugs are easier to quit. It is important that you come off drugs with medical supervision. Treatment programs are designed to help people come off drugs safely and work toward recovery and staying off drugs.

Many treatment programs teach skills for living drug-free.

You're Not Alone

The road to recovery is a long and bumpy one. Living a life in which you do not abuse prescription or OTC drugs will require a lot of hard work, as well as many changes to the way you live. You will need to look at the people in your life, and consider whether they will be able to help you stay clean. If they are people who encourage you to abuse prescription or OTC drugs, you may need to leave them behind and build new, healthier relationships. You will need to think about how you deal with stress, and the new ways you can cope with stress and bad feelings—healthy ways that don't include abusing prescription or over the counter drugs.

Relapsing Is Common

Relapsing, or starting to abuse drugs again after you've stopped, is a very common experience on the road to recovery. It is the norm and not the exception. This does not mean you have failed, or that you will never live without drugs. Relapsing is sometimes part of the process of learning to live your life in a new way.

Quit for Yourself

You stand a better chance of staying off drugs if you quit for yourself. You need to understand the reasons why you began taking drugs and what keeps you using them. Don't try to quit on your own—this is when you need a good support network.

Resources

You don't have to go it alone when searching for information on prescription and over the counter drug abuse. There are many information hotlines, websites, and books that you can trust. Look for books and websites that offer information and support that is nonjudgmental. Here are some trustworthy resources that can help you:

Books

The Science of Addiction: From Neurobiology to Treatment, by Carlton K. Erickson (New York: W.W. Norton & Company, 2007). This is a detailed but easy-to-understand book on brain science and addiction research.

Websites

Above the Influence
www.abovetheinfluence.com
This is an online resource that provides information about drug abuse (including illegal, prescription, and over the counter drugs), as well as information about resources that you can access. This website is written for teens and provides information to help make decisions about abusing drugs, addiction, and recovery.

KidsHealth
www.kidshealth.org
This website is written by health professionals and has separate sites for parents, kids, and teens. It has information about common side

effects of abusing prescription and OTC drugs, signs and symptoms of drug abuse, and what to do if you're worried about yourself or someone you care about.

National Institute on Drug Abuse
www.drugabuse.gov
This government website provides detailed information about classes of drugs, their side effects, symptoms of overdose and withdrawal, and signs and symptoms of drug abuse.

Organizations, Hotlines, and Helplines
Substance Abuse and Mental Health Service Administration (SAMHSA) (1-800-662-HELP)
(www.samhsa.gov)
This agency has a hotline and website and can help you locate treatment centers, help agencies, and counselors in your area. Their hotline operates 24 hours a day, 7 days a week and is staffed by compassionate and knowledgeable professionals who can help you take the first step in getting help.

Narcotics Anonymous
(www.na.org)
This website will give you information about the support systems that are available in your community.

Girls and Boys Town National Hotline (1-800-448-3000)
This is a 24-hour crisis line that is staffed by professional counselors. You can use this phone number if you are in crisis, or if you are looking for someone to talk with about your use of prescription drugs.

Glossary

acknowledging Accepting or admitting the truth of something

addiction Being physically or mentally dependent on a substance

ailments Minor illnesses

anxiety Feeling very worried, nervous, or uncertain about something

anxiety disorders Anxiety-related conditions diagnosed by a doctor

Attention Deficit Hyperactivity Disorder A behavioral disorder that includes the inability to concentrate or control actions

cells The functional and structural units of all living things

central nervous system The nerve tissues that control the activities of the body, brain, and spinal cord

chronic Persistent or difficult to change

crisis A time of great difficulty or danger

depression A medical condition in which a person feels sad and has difficulty functioning in life

dextromethorphan An ingredient in over the counter cough medications that is used recreationally to get high

dose A specific amount, or quantity, of medication

empathetic Able to understand and feel for someone else

excessive More than is necessary or needed

inappropriate Unsuitable or not right

insomnia Inability to sleep

intentional Done on purpose

legitimate Done according to the rules or law

meds Slang term for medication or drugs used for medical treatment

misuse To use something in the wrong way or for the wrong reason

panic attack A sudden and uncontrollable feeling of fear or anxiety

paraphernalia Equipment or things used to take or use drugs

perceive To look, see, or be aware of something in a certain way

rationalize To attempt to explain or justify something in a positive way

react Respond to something

receptors A tissue, membrane, or part of the body that responds specifically to a substance

reformulated Remade in a different way

relapse To return to a certain behavior

side effects A secondary, often unwanted effect of a drug or medicine

sulfa Sulfonamide, or a group of synthetic drugs

withdrawal Symptoms experienced when someone stops taking an addictive drug

Index

5/12